# Breaking Barriers

## Better Edition

Jason Criddle with Dr. Grace Cochin Psy. D.

You can find more of Jason's titles at JasonCriddle.com or
JasonTaughtMe.com All rights reserved.

ISBN-13: 978-1512291049

ISBN-10: 1512291048

# DEDICATION

I have a whole new motivation in my life. For the last few years, I have worked diligently to manifest the woman of my dreams. It really does work. I dedicate this book to my Emma, my Stephanie, and my Caiden.

# CONTENTS

# ACKNOWLEDGMENTS

Imagine how wonderful this world would be if every single person treated everyone else with love, respect, fairness, and compassion. Imagine. I would like to acknowledge every single beautiful human being on this planet. Without you, I would not be me. Without me, you would not be you. I love you all.

# EVERY GENERATION NEEDS A REVOLUTION

It is really damn weird to think about the fact that it is 2015, and we are STILL fighting, judging, and killing other human beings because of the color of their skin. That being said, energy is neither created nor destroyed—therefore, I do not feel much of the recent violence has as much to do with race as it does a few other things: boredom, labeling, our lack of progress or fulfilling a purpose as a species to name a few. We have a volatile amount of energy building within us, and this energy has been ready to explode or implode for some time. So, what is the difference between an explosion and an implosion?

We have had over 40 Presidents of these

good United States since the birth of our nation, but how many of those Presidents have created a drastic positive shift for not just our country, but all living beings on our planet and beyond? To understand a President or their cabinet, you would more or less need to understand the "game" that is our government, and the fact that the "system" we follow is based on a carefully constructed design by some very bright people. In addition, you should understand that this system was meant to change with time. I guess that could be read as a pretty bold statement, were it not for Thomas Jefferson saying, "Every generation needs a revolution."

Big deal, right? I mean, who was Thomas Jefferson anyway? It is not like he was a founding father, drafted The Declaration of Independence, or mandated our government to be run by the consent of the governed, not by the radical, secluded decisions of a group of people who are not taking responsibility for their actions. Our officials should not necessarily be held accountable for wrong doings, but should instead listen to the questions and concerns of the people— especially those who are ready to explode. The people causing "unrest" are not concerned with developing specific foreign or domestic policies. These "protestors" are merely lifting the veil of lies we have been spoon-fed for far too long. Their demands are about topics like cleaning our environment, income inequality, and ethics. But sadly, they are being silenced.

So what is an explosion? An explosion is a movement gone wrong. An explosion is a misunderstood attempt at a revolution. A large, peaceful group of people do indeed have a chance at creating shifts of change through organization and communication, but when "civil unrest" enters the picture, any attempt at a peaceful revolution is all but destroyed. Our unrest comes from a lack of unity, the boredom I spoke of earlier, and a "story" that is being told to those who will not take the time to educate themselves in our "new reality."

I not only believe Thomas Jefferson would stand at the forefront of some of today's more progressive movements, but I am also quite sure he recognized our "Unalienable" right to stand up and say, "It doesn't need to be this way." However, when the wrong people are running the "game," they strip away the power of the human spirit; they use our civil servants to protect their heinous agenda, all while using our public media to call REAL human beings names like *black*, *rioters*, and *criminals*. You have told three hundred million people to sit down, shut up, and don't even think about entertaining your rights as a citizen of this country, and you know what? They are listening. Alright, well, protesting is out the door. What do we do now?

That is where the implosion comes in. Though it is nowhere near as chaotic or volatile as an explosion, the damage can be just as devastating. That simple action is destructive, and if not directed from the standpoint of love and compassion, (rather than hate, misinformation, boredom, despair, or lack of purpose) even an overhaul of the human spirit can lead to somewhat explosive tendencies. If you want to have the greatest chance of any change, the change needs to come from within. Not from within a chosen few of us, but all of us. Enlightenment can no longer be seen as a luxury. Breaking down the body and mind to reveal the spirit is our ONLY true path to evolution and revolution. This process goes beyond color, borders, or religion—this process reveals the ONLY truth: you are God.

*"There is this falsified idea floating around that enlightenment is a pleasant and gratifying process. I can assure you, while some parts of it may be gratifying, enlightenment is an extremely destructive process indeed. Enlightenment is not an end game, it is simply a way to live your life. Enlightenment has nothing to do with becoming more loving, or better, or even finding happiness. Enlightenment is the crumbling away of lies. Questioning the façade of reality while emptying the mind of untruth. As a matter of fact, it can even be seen as the eradication of what we know as "truth." The "truth" about enlightenment is, it is painful. At times it is overbearing. You will experience more loss, despair, and turmoil on this path than you ever imagined you would experience.*

*It is your responsibility to grow. It is your responsibility to awe and be awed on this planet. The definition of awe is: a feeling of reverential respect, mixed with fear or wonder. It means you have just witnessed something so amazing, that it completely changes your paradigms and most complex of ideas. Your mind explodes in wonder and your soul is filled with joy as it begins to dance to new music and unheard of lyrics. You feel inspired (which means to breathe in spirit) to reach for new heights. We are so stuck in our habits, we have forgotten how to be* happy. How to find and fulfill our purpose. We have forgotten that God is within us all, waiting for us to ready our body for Him or Her to be awed through us. Every single moment can be a chance to change into who you are supposed to be.

Change comes from questioning. Questioning leads to more questioning, which reveals more truth. The process of the unveiling of truth forces you into enlightenment. Manifestation takes place simply because you are changing your thoughts and actions. Your mind automatically steers you in the direction you wish to go because you finally have a desire for a direction. However, we must become aware that there are no outside forces acting upon us. Everything that goes on in our life is a reflection of the choices we have made as well as our own outlook of ourselves. Until we are willing to change the way we feel about ourselves, our "external environment" may very well remain a constant. Whether you view your life to be positive, negative, or neutral, it may remain in a cycle and keep you from evolution or growth.

In essence, taking steps to understand the God Theory is about becoming something greater than any goal you can write down on paper… It is about what you become on the path to understanding. The God Theory is not an answer, it is just a point of view. It is a burning desire to have the things most are unwilling *to have by doing the things most are unwilling to do. Understanding the God Theory is understanding a lot of people may assume you are crazy. When people are confronted with information which questions their understanding, those stress hormones I mentioned earlier will flip back on and the body will revert back into defense mode. One of the most wonderful things about enlightenment is being granted the ability to no longer give a shit. Once you begin your path to becoming God, the universe becomes your canvas to manifest anything. All you have to do is decide."* – Understanding the God Theory

We must all take a moment to learn that the sun, the trillions of stars and galaxies, the trees, the birds, the whole of humanity—nothing is separate from God. We are not "humans" who witnessed the big bang—we ARE the big bang. Every single act of hate, fear, anger, violence, or abuse you willingly act out towards another with intent to harm, is ungodly. Every single one of us contain the will and freedom to express kindness, prosperity, and FOREGIVENESS to all who have ever brought us harm, intentionally or not. These ungodly acts only hurt us. We are keeping ourselves from evolving, and even if God were some external creation, he would have left us to clean up our own mess anyway.

It seems to me, our only option is to wake the fuck up and become better people.

# TEACHING COLORBLINDNESS

When I first wrote this eBook a year ago, I had just purchased Emma one of those DVD sets at the store that has 16 family movies from all different eras and directors. They were all filmed in the 70's and 80's, and I must admit, they were all pretty great. There were a few about dogs, a couple about life on the farm, bullies, bigfoot, unicorns, and even one about a little girl in an abusive family who ends up being rescued by a—wait for it—by a black man. The movie is called, *When I Find the Ocean.*

IMDB describes the movie as: "12 year old Lily Strickland has lost her father, a sailor, to the sea. She and her mother go to live with her grandparents. Lily and her family have little closure on the death of her father since he was never found, thus Lily sets out alone on a trek to the ocean to find the closure that she needs to heal her loss. Set in 1965 Alabama, during the Civil Rights marches."

In the opening scenes of the movie, a family is sitting at the breakfast table. The soon to be stepdad is reading some news in the paper and continually makes remarks about "those silly Indians..." and, "Well, you know those Indians can't be trusted."

The grandfather in the movie puts an immediate stop to this behavior. He tells the man, "There will be no cursing at my dinner table," then continues as he defends the Indian man being mentioned in the newspaper article. The grandfather claimed the man was, "by far one of the best trackers he had ever seen, on top of being a well-rounded good person." Of course, his act of defending such a good man leaves the racist, soon-to-be stepfather speechless, and the meal continues in the presence of a very pronounced uncomfortable silence.

Later in the movie, they introduce a scene to show how the little girl is physically abused by her soon-to-be-stepfather. This act causes her to run away from home, and only to get her leg stuck in a poacher's trap. When the poachers arrive and see a young girl in their trap, they start to perform awful acts on the girl. But luckily, a new friend comes to her rescue.

As the story progresses, the majority of the town goes on a manhunt for the both of them, believing the man to be a danger to the girl, as the poachers told a few bold-faced lies about the hero who came to her rescue. Throughout the movie, no matter where they are, they are treated terribly because the people in the small community do not understand why an older black man is walking around town with a young, white, teenage girl. There are even townspeople that go into the local gun and ammo shop to buy weapons for the sole purpose of putting the man "down". The woman at the shop practically gives out weapons to anyone who wants to hunt down this "deadly" black man.

As more is revealed about this hero's story, it is discovered that the people who are trying to hunt him down are the same people who killed his wife and children many years back.

These people burned his house to the ground with his family inside when he refused to let them force him off his own land. All because of the color of his skin.

Coming from an interracial family, racism has been prevalent in my life. Even now, when someone directly identifies another person by the color of their skin, I encourage them to take a more mindful approach. A label immediately causes us to compartmentalize everything we "think" we may need to feel about a person into some prepackaged lie—a lie completely based upon the perception of the person who implanted the label in your mind to begin with.

To this day, I work diligently to shield Emma's ears from bouts of hatred, racism, swearing, and negative speaking. I do not teach her to run from it, but rather, to be aware of it, to know that this hateful behavior generally comes from simple misunderstanding of effects one's words and actions have on others. I call her "colorblind" because she see the color of people's skin as their sole identifier. She simply sees people for how lovely, special, and beautiful they are as humans. She often holds the hands of my friends through grocery stores, at the malls, bookstores, or parks. She doesn't care at all about the color anyone's skin. If we bring a person into our lives, they are accepted and treated as family. Period.

One time, we were watching a movie with a "black" Santa Clause. She said to me, "That's not Santa Clause!"

When I heard this, I had an immediate strike of worry, not knowing exactly what was going to come from her mouth next. I asked her why she didn't believe that to be Santa. She remarked, "He is too skinny! Santa is fat!"

I instantly let out a sigh of relief. I then explained to her how we don't use the word "fat" to describe people, because such a word might hurt someone's feelings. For some reason (most likely because of political correctness and society's standards) teaching her about making fun of someone's weight did not seem as "bad" as teaching her about judging someone's skin color.

My mom taught us very early on that she did not care what the color of someone's skin was. Whether we were friends or dating them, all she cared about was us being around people who made us happy, people who possessed the will to treat others fairly. In my life, I have dated black, white, Persian, Indian, African, Asian, Hispanic, and any and all races in between. The color of someone's skin has never held any bearing or weight in my feelings towards them. To me, skin tone is just another beautiful expression of the art that is "the human." One of my friends asked me a few years ago, which women I think are the most beautiful. My response was, "All of them."

# ENCOUNTERS WITH RACISM

I remember my first day of kindergarten. We had this large area with shelves that held bins. This is where we would put our backpacks, school boxes, supplies, jackets, books, etc. This is also where all of the children would gather when entering or exiting the classroom. I was in the AM class, which ran from 9am to noon. There was a second kindergarten class that came in from noon to 3pm.

I don't really remember learning anything. I am pretty sure we just drew pictures, traced our hands, and made macaroni cards for our parents. The one memory that really sticks out from my entire kindergarten experience is a little boy named Steven.

The noon bell rang, which signaled to us kids that our parents had come to pick us up. Along with the rest of my classmates, Steven was standing by the bins with a large sheet of gold star stickers he'd brought to school. He was giving them out to all of the kids that walked up to him. Kid after kid would hold out their hand in anticipation of receipt of a gold star, then Steven would stick one on their hand. I, of course, ran eagerly up to Steven to claim my sticker. I held out my hand with a smile on my face, just to hear Steven say, "You can't have one."

When I asked, "Why?"

His response was, "Because you're black."

I didn't quite understand what he meant by this. I mean, I knew my dad had darker skin, and my mom had lighter skin, but I was just a child. The only response I could muster up was one of self-defense. I stammered and said, "Yes, but my mommy is white."

He looked at me a little puzzled and said, "Ok." Then he gave me a sticker.

As I walked outside and saw my mom standing there waiting for me, I started to cry. She embraced me before we walked to the car. Once we got home, she had a long talk with all of us about why people may say such things to us. She even warned me that this may not be the only time I encounter racism in school or throughout life. And believe me when I say that this wasn't our only racial encounter in school. My sisters and I were tormented often throughout the early years of our schooling. Bullied by children that didn't like us because of the color of our skin. We were told we were going to burn in hell, simply because we were "mixed breeds," and because my mom was a "nigger lover." My older sister received her own forms of punishment when a 5+ year rumor started about some nasty things regarding her sexuality. Of course, the rumors were just that—rumors. False. But that did not stop the pain she had to go through, pain that was brought on by someone labeling her for the color of her skin.

My parents were married for close to fifteen years. My dad was raised in Denver, Colorado and Corsicana, Texas; my mom was raised in a rural farm town in Georgia called

Moultrie. After my parents married, my mother's family completely disowned her. In the part of the country where she was raised, a white woman marrying a black man was completely unheard of, even in the 70's. Her family and friends wanted nothing to do with her since she had the nerve to marry a man of color.

I was about 8 years old before we made our first trip to visit her family. It is sad to think, the trip only took place because her family finally began to accept her, an acceptance that only came because she was taking steps to divorce my father. My mother's family was so happy for her departure from a fifteen year marriage, but for the wrong reasons. I also learned, even though they accepted my mother's return, few of our family members were thrilled at the chance of meeting "mixed kids."

Back then, the town had a population of less than 10,000 people. Even now, its numbers barely reach 25,000. As a child, walking into any grocery store in this town was like something out of a movie. As soon as the doors would open, allowing my sisters and I to step inside, everyone throughout the store would immediately stop everything they were doing to gawk at the "mixed kids" that were visiting their quaint town. I am certain this is what someone means when they say, "you could hear a pin drop." The air reeked of a thick, stubborn misunderstanding. People treated us like wild animals. They would pull their own children out of our paths and clear the aisles when we would walk down them.

Around 2010, I lived in Moultrie for almost 3 months. Even though the culture was more diverse as a whole, there still existed a level of segregation throughout the somewhat thriving town. I am sure you have heard of "the other side of the tracks." This town actually has a train track dividing it, separating one race of people from the other (though this may not be the case any longer). However, I did learn, most of the younger residents of this town would never think of promoting racism. It was mainly the older crowd, those who were unwilling to update their mindset through many generations of social change. Another major factor was the lack of leadership, the lack of people willing to stand up and say, "It doesn't need to be this way." All too often someone would cross the street or skip an aisle in the grocery store simply because I was standing there.

At our first family reunion, some members didn't show because we were attending. It was nice that my grandparents finally gotten over their bigotry. I was able to visit my grandfather once or twice before he passed away. My grandmother passed away around the time I turned twenty. We never had any significance of a relationship. Because of the way people treated us when we were children, I wasn't ever too excited about making the 24 hour drive just to be mistreated.

When I was 20, I dated a Hispanic girl. We drove to Georgia because my grandmother was laying on her death bed. My mother had already been by her mother's side for a few days and she needed me there for her. Before making the trip, my mom made sure I drew circles on the map around the towns we shouldn't stop in for any reason.

Over halfway through our trip, we stopped for gas in Alabama. We were far away from Selma, once of the places she told me not to stop. I pulled up and got out of the car. I started to head inside to pay for gas when the cashier ran outside to greet me. He was an older gentleman, and I could see the look of concern in his eyes when he nearly jumped out from around the counter to head outside to me. He asked me in a hurried manner, "How much gas do you need to get the hell out of this town?" He then explained: if anyone saw us at his station, we may not leave there alive.

He gave us ten dollars of free gas and pointed out a safe city on my atlas to stop and get more gas. He also informed me to look straight ahead if we caught any red lights. "And don't speed, cuz the cops will hurt ya. Get out of this town as fast as ya can." Looking back now, at this situation and others like it, I now see that this man was a guardian angel, at just the right place, in the right time—ready to look over us and save our lives.

A couple of years later, I would marry a "white" girl. We were head over heels for each other. She was scared, though, because her family was racist. No matter how much we cared for one another, she feared her family would disown her if they ever found out about me. Which is exactly what they did. They stopped at nothing to paint me to be a terrible person simply because of the color of my skin. We were married for less than six months before her dad made sure we got divorced. He drove to Dallas with a truck full of people to "rescue" his daughter when I was working one day. This action resulted in my apartment being cleared out, as well as my bank account. I lost my two dogs, my dignity, and my wife… all because of the color of my skin.

Even my best friend in high school had to sneak me into his house a few times before he ever told his parents about me. He told me they never allowed him to have friends of color, so he was worried about how they would react when meeting me. I remember his mom even joking around with me after a year or so of friendship with her son. She would often say, "I really like you even though you are black." And other times she would say, "Don't bring any of your brothers or sisters over here. One black person is enough." While these words were said with a smile, they were still coming from a biased place of fear or hatred. Luckily, his family would embrace "us all" (my family) sometime later, and we would all become one large family of friends for a few years. A funny side note, this same friend would later marry a girl that I dated in high school for no more than a month. We dated for such a short time because her father put a gun to my face when I walked into their home for the first time. He told me I didn't belong there, so I left.

# LEARNING TO LAUGH OFF
# CULTURAL IGNORANCE

Being the mixed kid, I was fortunate enough to hear all sides of racist jokes. I often hear, "Can I tell you a joke without you being offended?"

I learned at a young age to laugh off the jokes, no matter what. It is much easier to laugh than it is to become offended by something that really doesn't matter in the grand scheme of things, especially if it does not have anything to do with YOU. Someone making a statement out of pure hatred is much different than someone making a statement which pokes fun at the ignorance behind our lack of reasoning for racism. If you play the victim you will become the victim, so stand tall and keep smiling.

Since we can only understand the world from our own individualized perception, this would also mean, anything we say or do is a reflection of who we are. Hatred comes from hatred; someone saying something hateful out loud is saying it about themselves, not you. It's the same as someone telling a joke—they tell you the joke because it is funny to them. The simple act of telling you the joke is their way of gaining your approval for something they find humorous. I have, many times in my life stood up for others in racist and hurtful situations. However, a joke is a joke; life as a whole is sort of a joke. I like to believe life is a game, and how you play determines your reality. That is probably my reasoning behind finally breaking from my shell now, and printing some crude humor illustrations which poke fun at cultural ignorance.

I have spent a "little" time in the online dating arena, meaning, I have owned a dating site, started many for clients, and I have had profiles on dating sites before. While you would think most profiles consist of dreams, wishes, desires, and life goals, a good bit of profiles contain lackadaisical information.

Sadly, people just tend to speak about the things they hate or don't want in their life. Of course, this can tell you multitudes of information about someone's character. I have all too often come across someone who willingly types out in all caps, "I DON'T DATE 'SUCH AND SUCH' RACE." Or, "I don't date outside of my race." These same statements are usually prefaced with, "I'm not racist but…"

I have news for you: If the words, "I'm not racist but…" come out of your mouth, you are more than likely suffering from the same biased, ignorant behavior you claim to be dismissing within the same sentence. As D.L. Hughley joked in his stand-up, (paraphrasing of course) "I'm not racist, I've had 4 black people in my house." He then says, "If you know how many black people have been in your house, you are racist."

Ignorance is not a term I am using to offend people. Ignorance is simply a lack of knowing or even a desire to remain in the lack of knowing. Most people will shy away from learning about their own weaknesses or biases. But learning about all sides of your true self is a crucial step in reaching any form of peace or enlightenment on this plane. If you do feel the need to compartmentalize, judge, or label someone based on age, sex, race, creed, religion, etc., especially without having some sort of absolute experience to tie your bias to, you may wish to consider taking a long look in the mirror, and finally realize the entire world is a reflection of who you are. All people of all races are not just your brothers and sisters, they are you. Without them, you would not be you. And without you, they would not be them.

Of course, we can't BLAME others for this behavior. All we can do is hope others will, at some point on their journey, have the opportunity to open their eyes and allow self-healing to take over—even if it takes another 20 years, or even another lifetime, to do so. They learned this behavior from their parents, who learned it from theirs, who learned it from theirs and so forth. In just about every case I have seen, hate generally comes from generational or cultural ignorance. It's very rare to see someone who hates another for the color of their skin because of any justifiable reasons. Racism is never justifiable.

I owned a pool and landscape company

before the recession of 2008. Most of my employees were white. On numerous occasions, a homeowner would come out of their home, pass me by, and head over to one of my employees to start talking about the job, as if the employee were the owner of the company. I always figured I was passed because I was the dark skinned one working diligently in the flower beds. I even remember a customer of mine saying, "Oh, I thought you were just an employee because…" She stopped herself before continuing the sentence, but both of us knew what direction she was going. I had a chuckle about this for many days. I once again reminded myself, it is much easier to laugh than it is to become offended by something that really doesn't matter in the grand scheme of things, especially if it does not have anything to do with you.

.

# THE SCIENCE BEHIND RACISM
## -DR. GRACE COCHIN, PSY. D.

What is race? Commonly, race is divided into three different, general categories: Mongoloid (Asian), Negroid (African), and Caucasoid (European). Generically, the list of racial terms and slurs is almost unending. But these three categories, and any other term associated with race, neglect a wide range of human traits and characteristics that don't fall under the parameters of a certain "race." This again begs the question: what is race, really? What are the actual factors that determine race? Does being one race give you advantages over another? Above all, if race is such a common, inherent aspect of humans, why does *racism* (discrimination against another race) exist?

It may surprise you to learn that there is no scientific definition of "race" as it applies to humans. In fact, modern anthropologists no longer even consider race as an aspect of their research. This is because the scientific definition of race and the popular definition are completely different. While the latter may be based on the former, race is a misinformed idea that has been officially ruled out by the scientific community. That's right: modern science does not recognize that race exists among humans. But before we discuss the absence of race in current science, and what that means for "racism" in society, we must first look at the history of scientific racism.

*Scientific racism* is the term for using common scientific techniques to support the idea of racism. The roots of scientific racism can be found in Greco-Roman teachings. References to racial superiority have been discovered in writings as early as Hippocrates' *Airs, Waters, Places.* Favoritism towards and prejudices against certain peoples exist in teachings throughout the ancient world, in everywhere from China, to India, to Western Europe. Almost all cultures have at one point considered outsiders to be "barbarians," an early form of racism that was mainly rooted in fear of the unfamiliar. Early thinkers considered geography and climate to play a significant role in the physical appearance of different people. Greek philosopher Aristotle supported this belief; it is Aristotle who created the idea that natural creatures rest on a "ladder of perfection" according to their physical traits and skills. Though Aristotle did not specify humans on this scale, later scientists would use his ideas in support of their divisions between races.

In the 9th century, Afro-Arab philosopher Al-Jahiz tried to explain the origins of different skin colors, again citing the environment as the course. However, Judeo-Christian teachings refer more to their Biblical references. According to Christian thought, all peoples descended from Adam and Eve. In order to explain the multiple races and appearances between humans, the thought was further developed with the explanation that the three races (Mongoloid, Negroid, and Caucasoid) were descendants of Noah's three sons: Shem, Ham, and Japheth. This idea was heavily debated during the Enlightenment period, when philosophers and scientists were divided into supporters of monogenism (the idea that all humans descended from one source) and polygenism (the idea that humans may have multiple origins, thus multiple races).

Interestingly, before the Enlightenment thinkers of the 18th century, the words "race" and "species" were interchangeable in scientific writings. Even Charles Darwin, father of the Theory of Evolution, uses the term "race" as a synonym for "varieties" when discussing his findings. Darwin explains in further writings that these races, when isolated for long periods of time, do become different *species* of animal (the basis of this evolution theory). However, Darwin commented on the idea that human races connote distinct species of man. In his book, *The Descent of Man, and Selection in Relation to Sex*, Darwin explains his ideas on the theory of monogenism, the theory that humans all have the same origin:

It is impossible that the numerous, and unimportant, points of resemblance, between the several races of man, in bodily structure and mental faculties (I do not here refer to similar customs) should have all been independently acquired, they must have been inherited from progenitors who had the same characters.

But the idea that race connotes a distinction beyond skin pigmentation and geographical location remained prominent in scientific teachings. Writing around the same time as Darwin, scientist Johann Friedrich Blumenbach is credited with creating the five specific races: Caucasian, Mongoloid, Malay, Negroid, and American. Blumenbach based his theories on skull studies, stating that distinctions in skull shape, in addition to skin color and other physical traits, were able to divide the human species into different racial groups. Ironically, Blumenbach used this research to disprove the idea that Africans were inferior to other races in their health habits, natural talents, or mental capacities.

As everyone knows, racial inferiority and superiority has been a battle for millennia, of the most infamous in history are the slave trade and the Holocaust. The first was based on the idea that Africans are inherently less intelligent than the white European. In fact, some scientists of the slave-trade era claimed that Africans are genetically inclined toward subservience. This, and many other ridiculous notions, were extremely popular during their time, resulting in our own tragic history of slavery.

Perhaps an even more famous example of racism, though, is the Holocaust. Eugenics, or the belief in improving the genetic quality of a population, played a key role in the actions of the Nazi forces. Hitler and his scientists believed that the "Aryan race," based on typically Nordic traits such as blonde hair, petite features, and blue eyes, was genetically superior to all other races, particularly the "Jewish race." In an effort to "cleanse" the world of inferior genes, Hitler attempted to rid the world of the Jewish population, a "race" that is often still targeted by racist movements. Using scientific theories (which up to this point were still being taught), Hitler was able to influence entire countries of his ideas and cause a mass murder of nearly six million Jews.

After the horrors of World War Two, the theory that racism could be supported by science was formally denounced. In 1950, UNESCO released a statement known as "The Race Question," which officially rejected the scientific support for racial hierarchies and condemned racism. Drafted by Ashely Montagu, the UNESCO statement included the quote, "The biological fact of race and the myth of 'race' should be distinguished. For all practical social purposes 'race' is not so much a biological phenomenon as a social myth. The myth of 'race' has created an enormous amount of human and social damage. In recent years, it has taken a heavy toll in human lives, and caused untold suffering." At the time, this statement finally officially rejected the notion that different races hold different traits and talents.

Many scientists today still highly support this statement. While there is extensive evidence to support differing characteristics among various populations (which can be proven of any species), as early thinkers believed, these differences are heavily influenced by climate, geography, and group isolation. According to John. H. Relethford, author of The Fundamentals of Biological Anthropology, race "is a group of populations that share some biological characteristics... These populations differ from other groups of populations according to these characteristics." It is true that scientists divide many organisms into "racial categories" or varieties; these categories are determined by groups of organisms that have different genetic structures but similar backgrounds. This results from groups of organisms being completely isolated from their own species for thousands of years. Thus, they develop different traits to adapt to their environment (as Darwin initially pointed out in his own studies on group isolation and evolution).

However, humans tend to live in a wide range of environments over their lifespan, even traveling between environments often. While it is obvious that various group tend to have similar traits, (those that live in sunny environments tend to have darker pigmentation, for example) these traits are not different enough to completely categorize or separate these groups as a different species. Scientists across the board had noted that modern humans, *Homo sapiens*, have not been on earth for a long enough period of time to truly "evolve" from each other. Because of this, it is impossible to determine "racial categories" based on the same scientific data that has been collected among other species. Complete human isolation and total gene differences simply don't exist. The small differences in human populations are known to anthropologists as "ethnic groups," rather than races. This differentiates the scientific term of "race" from the colloquial term.

Researchers have conducted numerous studies on the links between race and traits such as intelligence or creativity, finding no significant differences that rested on skin pigmentation. Certain characteristics, such as blood type, have been seen to occur more frequently in certain populations of people, the same as pigmentation or bone structure. However, many anthropologists say that to associate ability with physical traits (in a group setting) is ridiculous. No scientific evidence has ever been found that links "race" to any kind of superiority, whether that be intellectual, physical, or anything else. Therefore, at least scientifically, the idea of "race" is a complete myth.

That being said, it is also understandable that science does not support the idea of *racism* is an inherent attribute. Many psychologists have completely ruled out racism as a human instinct. However, racism is undeniably real, and still prominent in our modern society. But if the concept of race among humans is scientifically incorrect, then why is racism a real factor in our lives?

The <u>real</u> science behind racism lies in the sociological and psychological effects on our brains. We are not immediately wired to be racist, instead, we learn traits of racism through our surroundings. Because of this, "instinctual" reactions to race form around this kind of learned information. It is the same as our fear of other animals, such as snakes or spiders. These fears do not naturally occur in our brains from the moment we are born. Instead, it is an experience or teaching that causes us to fear certain creatures, or even other humans. This is true for all animals – fear of the unknown is **not** instinctual. Rather, most animals, including humans, while precautious of the unfamiliar, are often more curious than fearful. It is only after an animal has a negative experience with, or is taught negative associations for an unknown, that they actually begin to fear it.

Interestingly, racism seems to have become an inherent, inescapable part of our society. Though we are not born with prejudice, the learned prejudices of our society are so deeply ingrained, that it almost feels as if we are instinctually biased. While racism is not an actually instinct, science has proven that unconsciously, most Americans are in fact racially biased, if not completely racist. Everything from job applications to crime rates are associated on some level with racial status. This "born racist" attitude of Americans is largely based upon what psychologists now call, "unconscious bias." Unconscious biases are based in stereotypes and prejudices that almost everyone learns simply by being a member of a society. While theses stereotypes are not directly taught in formal education, they are learned through interactions with other members of a society. And though a society may not admit to biases, theses stereotypes are often so deeply engrained within us, they only surface on what appears to be an "instinctual" level.

In most human interactions with confronting knowledge, there are three types of ignorance:

1. Things that we simply cannot understand, such as exactly how many neurons are firing in your brain every second.
2. Things we don't care to know or understand, such as the reason

someone's car is a different make or model than your own.

3. Things we don't want to know or understand, those unpleasant things that are uncomfortable to discuss.

Many psychologists put racism in the second and third categories. Most humans, as a part of our learned behaviors, don't care to become aware of our own biases. Which is one reason why racism is so prevalent in our society. For one, we do nothing to truly combat those who discuss their racist views, as the confrontation makes us uncomfortable. How often in the media have people been critiqued for bringing up race issues? Unfortunately, our reaction to the race discussion is more often a negative one. We just don't want to look at things that make us uncomfortable; the prevalence of racism in our society is one of the worst. For another, we don't want to recognize our own unconscious biases, as we believe that this makes us inherently racist. But does it?

The answer is no. Simply having these unconscious biases does not make someone a racist, per say. These biases are learned, unconscious thoughts that one develops based on the prevalent beliefs in a particular society. If you've grown up in an "all-white" neighborhood since birth, it is natural that you would feel uncomfortable in a prominently black area. This does not make you racist or prejudice, it simply makes you uncomfortable with unfamiliar surroundings.

Another term for these unconscious biases is "implicit racial biases," which, unfortunately, are all around us. But just how has science determined that we have these implicit biases? In many studies, researchers ask subjects to place words such as "happy," "sad," or "fear" into the categories of positive or negative. However, before the word is shown, a brief image of a black or white face is flashed on the screen. These studies have shown that when a black face is shown, people categorize the negative words much more quickly than positive words. The opposite was true for white faces. When subjects were shown white faces before the word list, the positive words were quickly categorized. According to Stanford University's research, "about 75% of whites and Asians demonstrated an implicit bias in favor of whites compared to blacks." Which means, that even though you may try to be non-racist, the bias is still there.

David Amodio, neuroscientist for New York University, conducted various experiments to test the limits and variations of implicit racial biases. His research supported many unconscious effects of these biases, but the four of the most noteworthy discoveries:

1. People tend to associate skin color with physical abilities over intellectual strengths.
2. People typically keep their distance from members of a different race.
3. A fact that should not be surprising to American voters, people tend to vote for members of their own race, regardless of political party.
4. Even doctors tend to treat patients differently; Amodio found that when given the same symptoms of a heart attack, doctors tend to favor white patients when prescribing clot-preventing drugs.

While these are not the only discoveries Amodio made in his experiments, they are quite unsettling. But what exactly did this neuroscientist find that *causes* these unconscious effects of bias? Interestingly,

Amodio noted that the area of our brain associated with implicit bias is, in fact, distinct from the areas that control self-regulation. Specifically, the area of our brain that "controls" our biases is called the *amygdala*, which is the part of our brain that is associated with fear conditioning. Thus, we do not "choose" to be racially bias. Instead, our stereotypes are learned from our environment on such a deep level, that they become reflexive in the same manner as the fear of spiders or heights.

The key though, between being truly racist and merely having learned biases, is how you behave based on these unconscious thoughts. The amygdala is associated with unconscious reaction, however, it does not have complete control over our behavior. The highly complex prefrontal cortex holds the real control, allowing us to inhibit impulses and make complicated decisions. While the amygdala makes us inherently *bias*, it is our prefrontal cortex that determines whether or not we are truly *racist*.

So what does this mean for our society, if we have the ability to control racism, but allow it to still run rampant? The answer: we are human. The prefrontal cortex is an incredible part of our brain, allowing us to make decisions and control our instincts. However, the prefrontal cortex only controls what you think, not how you think it. It is completely your choice whether or not to believe and act on your implicit biases. When asked if racism will ever disappear, Dr. Robert Sussman, a physical anthropologist and author of *The Myth of Race: The Troublesome Persistence of An Unscientific Idea,* said to The Huffington Post:

I am not sure if racism will disappear in the U.S. or in Europe. It is so intensely a part of our culture. However, we can make it disappear in a major portion of our population. To do this, we must continue to teach our children (and adults as much as possible) the realities of what the concept of race is, and how it is totally incorrect biologically. The way to do this is to teach about the history of the concept of race and racism, how it developed over the past 500 years, and what it really means. People can and do understand the reality of genetic variation and how this can be extremely good for the population, and for individuals. Sometimes people do bad things – like the Nazis – but these were learned (though they developed with certain motives in mind) and are not inherent, genetically determined behaviors.

What people do depends upon their history, their background, their neighbors, and not upon the biological reality of race! After all, variation is the spice of life!!

Unfortunately, it seems we may never be rid of racism. Though science has officially declared "race" among humans a myth, the damage of this idea has already been engrained in our minds. Even if you live in an ethnically diverse environment, there is a high chance that you still have these implicit biases on some level. And that is nothing to be ashamed of. However, it is your choice in how you handle these biases. If you recognize your biases and try to combat them in your daily life, then you are already ahead of the game. The first step is recognition. Try to find out what triggers your own biased reactions. Once you determine the factors, you can more easily make an informed choice on how you behave.

## HOW CAN WE CHANGE OUR
## PERSPECTIVE?

Well that is simple: by learning we all have a unified purpose here on Earth. Not just the singular purpose of you, the individual reading this book, but all of us. We need to come to the understanding that we are in fact, one people. We are all part of the same consciousness, and it takes every single one of us to make the world go round. If every thought and action of one directly effects the thoughts and actions of the whole, can you not take a moment to understand exactly how your own thoughts and actions touch the lives of every single person on the planet? On your good days, your moments and experiences with others reverberates your emotional state, your love or hate, your biases, feelings, and attitude, regardless if you are aware of it or not. Any person you come in contact with will take this energy from you, and exchanges it with another, and another, and another, and the other party in the exchange, passes on your same energy to another, and another, and it continues to millions, and even billions of people. So, what about your bad days? Your bad feelings or bad attitude, how do you think these directly effect the world?

I am not one to watch sports. I am not one to watch television at all, really. If I do sit down and watch something, it may be the occasional movie with my daughter. Sometimes, a friend will recommend a show or a series. While I do like to sit down and relax, I will get an episode or two into the show before I realize that there is more important work to be done. Then, the show never gets finished. MY show MUST go on.

I remember the last football game I watched. When I say watched, I mean, glimpsed upon. I was at a restaurant with Emma, and since I do not allow her to watch TV in restaurants, I purposely sat across from the big screen on the wall opposite, our table. I must admit, the TV caught my eye quite a few times, especially since the commotion on the TV corresponded with the actions, screams, boos, and cheers of the restaurant patrons.

At this particular moment, it appeared a play had just finished, a penalty was called, and the offensive line was gathering in a huddle. The spectators of the game did not seem very satisfied with the play. The same people cheering on their favorite team just a moment ago were now screaming and crying out in anger—not just here in the restaurant, but even the ones in attendance at the game. Of course, the team ignored the cries and anger of the crowd. They were there to play the game for themselves and their families— probably because of their own drive, tenacity, and passion for the game. While I am certain a part of a professional athlete could very well be playing the game "for the fans," I do not believe for one second that the players play the game to satisfy the egos and ill opinions of those in the crowd—those who would never have the gumption to stand in the huddle or play the game themselves. This is why the huddle fascinated me. So much stillness amidst the chaotic havoc that is football.

Being in Dallas, I am certain you can imagine, the Cowboys were playing. I don't remember who they were playing though. Not because I am not a football fan, but because I was NOT watching the game consciously. As far as who I am a fan of, I will just call myself a free agent. I don't watch enough sports to cheer for one team.

Now this all may seem just a little strange, because most people don't watch a football game for the huddle. Just as people don't watch a basketball game to watch the players run to the sidelines to get directions from their coach. The average person is viewing the game to watch the results of the huddle, or the outcome of the huddle. I was so fascinated by the huddle, that I continued watching the game specifically for the next huddle.

I also noticed there was only one person talking in the huddle. The quarterback. He gave the directions to everyone on the team. No one argued. No one refused to run the play. None of the team felt the need to cry out in anger because of the results (or lack thereof) of the last play. The QB gave directions and the team listened. Everyone knew their place, their purpose.

When the team broke, everyone headed to the line of scrimmage, and they did so in such an orderly fashion that it was almost beautiful. No one had to stop and ask for directions again. No one had a change of mind or a change of heart. Everyone knew their place, their purpose.

They ran the play. The formation of both lines almost mirrored that of the last play, the center hiked the ball, and the QB backed up in preparation for a long throw instead of handing it off for a run as they did in the previous scrimmage. The receiver caught the ball around his own eighteen yard line, and never looked back—he just kept running. The play was a success. Dallas received a touchdown, and the once belligerent, angry, fans were rejoicing in happiness once more. The field and the players were still only acting out of instinct, and stillness.

Then I got to thinking about the quarterback. The position as a whole and the value a captain (or anyone who knows their purpose) can offer their team, regardless of their religious preference or skin color. But, it dawned on me. Even though this quarterback was a captain and a leader to everyone in the huddle, he wasn't even the one calling the shots. He had a microphone in his helmet and he was taking directions from someone else. Sure, he is the captain on the field, but the captain of the game? No, too was just playing his part on the bigger picture. His purpose is to put into action, the plays that are being called from the coach on the sidelines.

Is the coach running the show? Surely he knows a little bit about how to play the game, right? Not to mention, the coach can see the entirety of the contest from a $3^{rd}$ party, unbiased perspective (if he chooses to remain unbiased of course). He can see the offense and defense of both teams without being directly involved in the chaotic havoc of the field. He even has "special" teams of people with their own individual expertise who can watch specific players on the field and feed him critical information to assist in his efforts of victory. He can help in the elimination of errors by responding proactively to situations before they happen, and plan ahead. Later in the game, this could eliminate the faulty placement of a "wrong" play, based off of an irrational or emotional reaction to something.

He can pave the way for the whole team to achieve victory, as each individual player is more than likely focusing on their own victories. His purpose is to be there for his team.

Even though it may seem the coach is orchestrating "certain victory" from the sidelines, he too has a microphone with a voice whispering (or I guess they could be shouting) directions, suggestions, and intel into his ear. With all of his knowledge and the support of all his assistant coaches, he still has to deal with the spectators. As calm as the field may look, as focused as the team may seem, there is still chaos with which he is dealing, especially with tens of thousands of screaming fans at his back.

Sometimes you need someone uninvolved. Someone sitting up high. Someone with a much broader perspective. Someone drowned in stillness. In the calm of being. Someone who can look down at all he surveys, all he has created, even in the presence of the opposition. This is the owner. The owner of the football team really only has a few responsibilities. However, they may be the most important ones of all. The owner's job is to create. The owner's job is to provide for. The owner's job is not to lead followers, but to amass a legion of leaders. The owner realizes, to run such a substantial, carefully managed organization, he cannot do his job on his own. But, I would be willing to bet, he has the ability to make people believe in him. I would be willing to bet, if he lost it all, he would have the knowledge to create something even more magnificent the second, third, or billionth time around, simply because he knows his purpose.

But what of the spectator? What causes someone to lash out? What causes someone without any direct involvement in the game to lose all emotional resiliency in the name of a silly contest? After all, you have heard me say it before, "you can tell the size of a man by the size of the problem he allows to bother him." I do not believe the game of football is silly; I am certain it is hard as hell. I played a bit in middle school, lol. Yes, I said lol in my book. Even moments ago, I was watching a summer training camp video for the Auburn Tigers (to get ideas for leg workouts at the gym tomorrow) and it was grueling and painful just to watch. I feel blessed to know I may have done even a tenth of that workload when competing in Crossfit. Those guys were beasts. As I said, I do not believe the game of football is silly, but I do believe having a manic personality episode during a game you are watching is a little silly, especially if you are one of those who would never have the gumption to stand in the huddle or play the game themselves. That does not mean people cannot celebrate or be disappointed while watching a game. As a matter of fact, there is nothing wrong with being a spectator at all, because even the spectator is a master of their own domain. The spectator possesses a wonderful gift that they too can share with the world. The spectator is not a spectator, because "spectator" is just a label. The spectator has a purpose to fulfill too, and even the act of watching the game is part of their ultimate purpose.

The person sitting in the farthest seat, at the highest point in the bleachers, still needed to purchase the ticket in order to create a sold out game. Without everyone participating, there would be no football game at all. From the fan to the player, the owner, the coaches, the concession attendants, the person who installed the red light you hit at the corner of 5th and Broadway on the way to the game, the great, great, great, great grandniece of the woman who baked a loaf of bread for her family a hundred years ago, and their dog, every single one of us are connected. Every single one of us are part of a unified purpose. This is life. This is oneness in its truest form.

Imagine looking at a pool table and seeing the red ball, as it sits next to the side pocket. Cause and effect teaches us, if I hit the cue ball, and the cue ball hits the red ball, the red ball will go into the pocket. This however, is a skewed and very simple understanding. In actuality, when you hit the cue ball, and the cue ball hits the red ball, and the red ball goes into the pocket, that very scenario needed to take place in order for the ENTIRE universe to remain in existence.

We are all one people and one consciousness. Many call it God, others call it Allah, while some call it Source. There are many names for the light that lies within us, but one thing is for sure, when our sun rises in the morning, it doesn't rise on just one race, religion, or even a one particular group of people with so-called "normal" sexual preferences... our sun shares its light with all of us.

Having an awareness of your own consciousness helps you to realize your purpose and the purpose of others in your life. While it may sound like a simple feat, awareness will take you a lifetime of practice. I have come to learn, anyone who comes into your life carries with them an unlimited opportunity for growth and change, so meet as many people as you can; get out of your house, talk to strangers, dance with someone in an elevator. If you feel you are being restricted by someone in your life, or even an action or thought of your own doing, let go. Imagine life from the other side. If it's no longer serving you, let it go. Selfish? No. You are aware of your purpose and it is your responsibility to make all of your decisions based on that purpose. If you are doing nothing with your life, expect nothing to find you. Manifestation will help you find a direction, but you still need to be "doing" or "becoming" something for "it" to find you.

There is a universal love that guides us all, though we have to become aware of our own power to experience this love on an ongoing basis. This love is God, living its life and purpose through us, and even God can only be realized or perceived through an individual's consciousness, which means, that person's powers of manifestation, attraction, or even God is predicated upon their own level of awareness.

It's your life. What are you going to do with it? Who are you going to answer to? Do you feel you should dive deeper and deeper into your inner being to discover God's potential? The potential that has been lying dormant within you? Or should you continue living a miserable life, a life pushing you to your own breaking point? Answering to people who feel you should be blessed at the opportunity to deal with the grief they are willing to give you. Spouses, family members, or even bosses who are consistently unappreciative of your desire to become a better person.

God is in an effortless attempt to take judgment away from us. Though we must prepare ourselves to be in the right frame of mind to do so. Self-realization takes a willingness to change, and most just do not feel they need to change. We are bombarded now with new ideas: religion, philosophy, theology. People get into arguments about various perspectives and tell others they are wrong for believing what they believe. They cast biased judgment based upon ignorance of the unknown, having never walked in a single other person's shoes, never having to grow up in another's household, with another's parents, morals, values, addictions, delusions, dreams, ambitions, problems, and inhibitions.

Have you ever taken a moment to wonder: are they all correct in their beliefs? Not just one of those people, but all of them? The human mind will always find what it is looking for (once a decision has been made), which means the human mind also creates its own belief system based upon its own experience of reality. God is everything that is and is not reality. "Truth" is deep within the beholder's perception of reality. There can be no one single truth to existence—there can only be a point of view.

Could we not say we are being bombarded with multiple truths because multiple truths are "it?" "It" meaning *reality*? Should we not let go of judgment and accept it? After all, we cannot change another's perception by simply having a perception of our own, so there is no reason to judge anyone. Instead, we should have a desire for understanding, especially for those who are different from us, or even those who have done us wrong. You are both the bearer of the apple and the serpent. Until you relinquish your desire to judge, control, and identify reality as "good" or "bad," your life will more than likely remain in its cycle of regression.

We experience life as a narrative through our singular consciousness perspective called, "I AM." This feeling of "I AM" exists in every single conscious creature in existence. Even though this timeline is experienced through individuals, we are all still a piece of that single unified consciousness called God. The "consciousness" is developed within the human mind, which creates its external reality by the integration of relationships between the energy and information output of the unified consciousness, tuning into the individuals memories, emotions, and physical body. The output or result of this process is what we experience as time, space, and matter. We experience this reality linearly because it is the only way the human mind can comprehend the sheer magnitude of information available to us. The mind does not "discover" information; the person discovers information and the mind tunes into infinite consciousness to manifest the person's desire(s).

It would seem, if the word of God was in fact written in a book, it wouldn't have stopped two thousand years ago. The word of God would be written in text throughout the entirety of our lives. Not to mention, text, and even the gift of reading, were not skills most people possessed hundreds of years ago. It was an art, and look at all of the artists of today. Look at the abundance of creativity that surrounds us all. Original fabrications, art, new dance styles, music, software, and life-changing technology that shapes our lives before we are even aware it exists... all here because someone actually followed through on an idea and took it to completion. The story of EVERYTHING cannot possible by inside one book, it would seem *everything* would be the evidence of everything.

When we say, it's raining outside. It's snowing. It's cold. It's awesome. It's painful. It's beautiful. It's amazing... "It," is the closest thing we have to describing what we would know and believe as God. "It," is a creation of our ideas and perception. So rather than always being in a search for truth, we should spend even more time searching for the God within ourselves. Letting go of racism, hate, false beliefs, and ideas which spread fear, ignorance, and misunderstanding bring us more truth than Google and YouTube ever could.

You see a tornado rip through a neighborhood and both the homes of the believer and non-believer are destroyed. The white man and the black man. The gay, the straight. This is reality. This is God. This is non-judgment in its truest form. God is chaos, setting the stage for us to bring peace to our own reality, no matter what circumstance is brought before us. God is also the peace within us that is ready to lend a helping hand to another person who lost their house, even though we have lost our own. God is the everything of the everything.

Even if we were to try to understand this force, this "it," we wouldn't come close. We can't possibly comprehend or see "it." Even if we did experience "it," there would be no "it," because "it" would only be a manifestation of what we would believe our perceived experience to be. It is God, materialized in matter, giving us an opportunity in this lifetime to spiritualize that matter with a loving, compassionate, contemplative, forgiving, knowledgeable perception.

Reality is the cause and effect of life, just as life is the cause and effect of reality. Trees growing, birds chirping… everything else on the planet is living its purpose while we allow everything else's purpose to keep us from doing what we want to do, being who we want to be, or living as happily as we wish to live. We cast judgment, we don't forgive people, and we remain in a state of darkness. Why? Because of cultural ignorance. We have forced ourselves to detach; we have forced ourselves to remain in a state of unknowing. Nature doesn't hurry or worry, yet it turns out fine. That is because nature let's go. Nature has become "it," while we have separated ourselves from "it."

The chaotic behavior of life, our truth, is necessary in order for the opposite (duality, relativity) to exist. Your stress must happen to experience happiness. But even distress (negative states of being) has its adversary, eustress. (A constructive state of stress: meditation, cardio, weight lifting, yoga…) Not only is eustress a word that no one has ever heard of, it is also necessary for growth. Death must happen to appreciate and experience life, just as a crisis is sometimes necessary for someone to appreciate and experience life. Breaking down is sometimes necessary for reconstruction, and enlightenment is all about surviving various stages of deconstruction and reconstruction. $3^{rd}$ dimensional consciousness was created for education and we are here to fill our bodies with knowledge—all so we can observe ourselves as God's essence. God made this dimension to see and reflect upon itself in action, and we are God in action.

# LIFE AFTER 9/11

A few years ago, on a Sept. 11ᵗʰ anniversary, I made a post online saying, "Remember the peace, not the pain." Humans are generally very compassionate people; whenever there is a massive tragedy, we always seem ready to lend a helping hand. For a few days after the attack, I remember how peaceful the entire world seemed. Firefighters were driving through neighborhood streets with their lights flashing, and people would stop just to honk and wave. People were driving the speed limit. Others were saying "please" and "thank you," holding open doors, smiling at strangers, and allowing shoppers to cut in line at the store. For just a few days, it seemed like the entire world was "waking up." This, of course, was a state of denial, phase of the five stages of grief. The next stage is anger, which is brought on by fear, and the media made sure to scare the shit out of everyone after our brief period of peace. The first couple of days after the incident, no one really knew what was going on, but once the media started pointing blame and labeling, the fear and anger grew.

There were attacks on innocent grocery store owners, convenience store clerks, and taxi cab drivers. Not only were laws changed, and "Patriot" acts put in place, nationwide security and surveillance hyped up, racial profiling began running rampant. This country turned a blind eye to the very moral fabric which binds our constitution, declaration, and bill of rights. So-called "random" security checks were being issued out at airports just for the harassment of anyone that looked of Middle Eastern decent. Attacks, muggings, and robberies of innocent American Citizens would become a permanent presence on the tube and the net. Thus, the age of desensitization began.

Our misplaced fear is responsible for the evil acts we do to others. Judgment, lies, hurt, using people—all of these behaviors stem from our ignorance or lack of knowing our true self. Circumstances which test our courage and overall good nature will also test our willingness to remain ignorant. It is our duty to become aware of our evil acts, our fears, and even the pain we have caused others. Again, this destruction of lies and untruth will allow you to open yourself to the true wholeness of your highest self. Once you become aware, you are faced with a decision—a decision to keep becoming your best self, or to stay the weak, angry, depressed person you were yesterday. Not just once, but every second of every day.

All of this anger and race nonsense aligns itself perfectly with the "storm" we seem to be dealing with today. On one side, you have one race marching with guns in the street and no one doing anything to stop them. On the other side, you have another race of unarmed people being gunned down outside their own homes. In the middle of it, you have "viral" videos plaguing the internet as the very fabric of our once great nation gets burned away without notice. While real world problems are being played out step by step in front of our very eyes, we distract the masses with drills of military exercises and police brutality—just to help keep the populous from thinking on its own. That said, I am not an advocate of brutality of any sort. Unfortunately, human beings are the only species on earth capable of performing such atrocities against one another. I will also say, I am an advocate of the police.

Police officers have to be some tough ass people. They should be given respect simply because their duty is to wear the badge and uphold the law, without prejudice. A police officer, domestically, is usually the only shield standing between an innocent life and a threat from someone with intent to harm. Do you think they do it for the paycheck or because they felt a higher power calling them to service?

The news will ALWAYS reflect the most evil shit society has to offer. Why? It is their job. But that does not mean you have to feed into it. As citizens, I don't believe it is our duty to take these grotesque videos and images from the most infrequent and inhumane acts we can find in our streets, and strew them across social media for all to see. This action does nothing expect promote more fear and violence and it has the ability to halt anyone who wants to take a stand for change. Instead of saying things like, "police state" and "fuck the police," perhaps you should think about telling a cop "thank you," shaking one's hand, or buying them a meal. Police officers are not the antagonists—we are. We are a silly race of fear-driven people who feel so out of control, we pay a salary to members of our own society to police ourselves. In the grand scheme, our police are being played as pawns by the same people running the "game."

Anytime a "real" problem pops up in the news, it usually gets overshadowed by a story of some celebrity death or DWI. But nowadays, it seems "police brutality" videos are all the rage. The prevalent information becomes yesterday's news and people begin to look the other way. In turn, society becomes more and more confused and disconnected. Our views become more distorted as we turn the other cheek at situations where we should be standing up for our fellow human beings. Having a voice on the internet is much easier than in real life, but it is high time we change that perspective.

Forgiveness is knowing that every single

circumstance you have ever faced in your life had to happen in order to create the wonderfully complicated person you are now. If someone says or does something to upset you, just remember, it has nothing to do with you, and it definitely has nothing to do with the color of anyone's skin. Nothing. You can freely live your life and purpose completely unaffected by the hate of others. To say outside circumstances have no influence on our inner being is silly, however, circumstances can only affect us as much as we allow them to. If you are grounded in the present, and walking along your path with the God that swells (waiting to break free) within you, there would be no reason for fear, anger, lack of love, unhappiness, or even the lack of a willingness to forgive.

We have chosen a life of seclusion and isolation. I said on a radio show a few weeks ago that it is difficult for us to love unconditionally because we never experienced it ourselves. Sadly, more people of my generation grew up in situations far worse than I could ever imagine. But in order for us to stop labeling others and segregating our bodies and minds from our brothers and sisters, we MUST awaken. There is no global awakening, just an individual awakening on a global scale. It is up to all of us to spread our stories of strife to help bring others strength. The separation of light and dark is merely knowing and unknowing. Unknowing is ignorance, while the opposite is God. God is the knowledge you seek, need, and crave. God is "it," and you are surrounded by "it" awaiting your acceptance of truth.

Like the good doctor said earlier:

"In most human interactions with confronting knowledge, there are three types of ignorance:

1. Things that we simply cannot understand, such as exactly how many neurons are firing in your brain every second.
2. Things we don't care to know or understand, such as the reason someone's car is a different make or model than your own.
3. Things we don't want to know or understand, those unpleasant things that are uncomfortable to discuss."

While many doctors may believe racism falls in between categories 2 and 3, I believe our lack of desire to face our problems would fall into a very unpleasant "4," all on its own. Things we refuse to discuss because we were taught to sweep real problems under the rug.

Our ignorance stems from fear and anger, and fear and anger leave us in hell. We are all so afraid to face the truth because we were taught to smile through the pain and not face the real problems that plague us on an individual, or even global scale. Enlightenment teaches us, there is solace in the pain. Facing your biases, your fears, your "buttons" that others can press, this is the true path to enlightenment. I said once before, "vulnerability gives you power."

As a species, we cannot possibly seek peace or salvation, or whatever spin you prefer to put on it, until we choose to put our minds and bodies in motion to receive it. "It" always comes back to choice. Nothing will change until YOU make a decision to change. Once YOU become better, the rest of the world will follow suite. Spend the remainder of your days promoting peace, not ignorance. If you are not going to hold my hand while we break down the barriers holding us back from becoming GOD, from becoming better people for our planet, then hold someone's. We have a lot of work to do.

**"The only thing necessary for the triumph of evil is for good men to do nothing." – Edmund Burke**

# ABOUT THE AUTHOR

"Jason Criddle Is a rare mind. I have never met anyone in my life with the knowledge he possess. No matter what your problem or worry may be, he always seems to know exactly what to say. I am proud to say he is my friend, my mentor, and my coach. Were it not for him, my life would not at all be what it is today. Take the lessons he teaches to heart, and use them to change your own piece of the world."

– Ranae Smith, student of Jason Criddle

Please visit JasonCriddle.com

www.ingramcontent.com/pod-product-compliance
Lightning Source LLC
Chambersburg PA
CBHW050508290526
45786CB00006B/2491